exploited labor

exploited labor

poems by

Amber Awni

Published by Rainbow Raven Publishing LLC

Paperback ISBN 979-8-218-34032-2

Cover Art by Katarina @nskvsky on Fiverr

this book is dedicated to all mothers

especially to those battling
prepartum/postpartum depression

may this book shine a light for you on your dark
days

author's note

hello & thank you so very much for buying this book.

before we continue this journey together, i wanted to say a few words:

art is, and has always been, a rebellious voice against the status quo.

this world is slowly but surely losing art in all forms— movies remade over and over again, architecture around us becoming bleak, color bleached from anything except for advertisements—

artists,

writers,

painters,

illustrators,

sculptors,

all creatives alike,

are not making enough money to justify creating—so they stop completely.

i want you to think for a moment, what do you do when you come home from work every day?

turn on a show, read a book, listen to music, play a video game, bust out a canvas?

humans turn to art, in some form or another, whenever we possibly can.

in art, we find solace, identity, comfort.

in art, we find ourselves.

please, be an ally to artists—authors included.

if, for whatever reason, you do not enjoy this book (or any book, for that matter),

please donate it to your local library instead of returning it.

(you can always tear me a new one in your review)

i am, like you, a human being living under capitalism, and writing books is my livelihood.

★★★

thank you, dear reader.

★★★

table of contents

{spoon fed}

★★★

/ i saw beauty / in the sleeping princess / awaken from /
a single / kiss / play the tape / of my story / forward / &
as a 23-year-old / i found my 30-year-old / best friend /
in my bed / after i had fallen asleep / alone / how long
was i taught / to calmly accept advances / from men /
that i did not / consent to /

★★★

To the raven-haired   princess   that accepted
        the liar's love   after all:

            I understand.   I only see   the
                good   in people, too.

★★★

we watch cartoons from a young age seeing the narrative
of these young maidens suffering in the place they're in
we see the princes glorified to shine but without their
own elbow grease galloping in on a steed to save them
take them away to their castle to live happily ever after
look again these women could live their lives
independently but the men they fall for have no life-skills
they can't clean a house they can't cook a meal and they
have never worked a day in their life the morale of the
story is even royalty outsource their incomplete work to
their future daughter-in-law

★★★

work experience

$8.00   <u>2010</u> $7.25

I got my first job today! I'm working at that Halloween
warehouse in Canoga Park—you know, the one that is
open year-round? They're hiring for the month of
October and even though I don't turn 18 for another
week, I feel like I'm acing this adult thing.

★★★

$8.00   <u>2010</u> $7.25

I've been dating this guy, and like, I *really* love him. But
I also get this feeling he doesn't love me the same way—
and even though he's a little bit older than me and still
doesn't have a job and lives with his mom, he's *really*
good at playing drums and I am easily played—I push
people away when I'm scared they will leave at some
point, like digging my nails into an egg-shell and
expecting it not to break, and I'm always surprised by the
mess I have to clean up afterwards.

★★★

$8.00   <u>2010</u> $7.25

It's the second night of October and I'm throwing a party
for my 18th birthday—my boyfriend shows up for like 10
minutes? Later, when I'm filled with liquid courage and
on the verge of puking, I text him it's over.

★★★

$8.00   October 28th, 2010 $7.25

I think I'm dying. I wake up from a nap before one of
my last shifts at the Halloween store, and I can't seem to
get out of bed. Sitting up feels like trying to bend a stick
past its breaking point—I feel like I will pop into pieces if
I keep trying. It takes me hours, but I make it to the
Emergency Room and wouldn't you know, I'm
pregnant. Turns out, you *can* get pregnant on birth
control.

★★★

$8.00   2010 $7.25

I didn't know it would be so hard to play God.

★★★

$9.00   2010 $7.25

I landed a job at a grocery store that I have literally never
shopped at. Also, I have no idea what I'm doing and the
guy training me knows it. He's a literal wizard. The rest
of the crew remind me of what a freakshow would be:
accepting.

★★★

$9.00   2010 $7.25

I'm a creek. Flooding is not supposed to happen this early
in the season—I bring my leaking vessel to the hospital.

★★★

$9.00   2010 $7.25

I am lying in the hospital bed and wondering if you will look like your father.

★★★

$9.00   December 10th, 2010 $7.25

Where other women hold life in this room, I hold Death. He's beautiful.

★★★

$9.00   2011 $7.25

I have my first review a month after losing him. I don't get a raise. I am told *"we almost let you go, but we decided to give you a chance—"*

                         I should have asked for that in writing.

★★★

$12.10   2013 $7.25

Can someone please explain this thing called a wage gap to me?

★★★

$12.75   2014 $7.25

Working for large companies truly makes you feel the pinch of pennies with every step—

workwithasenseofurgencythecustomersare waiting

★★★

$13.40   <u>2015</u> $7.25

Did you know women can experience postpartum depression after pregnancy loss?

★★★

$14.05   <u>2016</u> $7.25

Have you ever heard of prepartum depression?

★★★

$15.35   <u>2018</u> $7.25

Do you know what it feels like to have to choose between your child and your job?

★★★

$16.00   <u>2022</u> $7.25

If I have learned to dance with a cart better than a person, does that make me talented, or taken advantage of?

★★★

$16.00   <u>2022</u> $7.25

Do you know what an at-will employer is?

★★★

$10.00   2022 $7.25

"How can I help you today?"

★★★

"wifey material"

like that's all

our worth just

some piece

of fabric made

for men to

rub their bodies

on like the term

is geared towards

endearment not as

a tool for boyfriends

to manipulate their

girlfriends hold them

accountable for becoming

their vision of a real

woman but heaven forbid

the girls hold men

accountable at all

but haven't you heard

men are dogs

that phrase does not mean

                                    what you think it means

                                    it is only part of a warning

wise old women would once

whisper to their daughters

                                    like dogs men should

                                    be bred or put down

depending on their nature

how many more girls and

                                    women must be cut

                                    down before we listen

NoT aLL MeN

the ideal wife knows / how to smile / like a beauty
pageant winner / but only when you tell her to / the
ideal wife laughs / a bark / for your misogyny / the ideal
wife gives / you the clear / for locker room talk / for
picket-fence fury / for every indiscretion / she has to
bleach / behind closed doors / scrubbing away / stained
insecurities / & any carpet-covered violence / the ideal
wife / does not mind / she does not think / for herself /
she is / Artificial Intelligence / the ideal wife cooks /
your favorite meals / but she herself never gains weight /
she has no appetite / she shuts her mouth / like a bear
trap / never speaks up / for herself / she knows / not to
speak / unless spoken to / the ideal wife is / submissive /
she does not hold grudges / she does not nag / the ideal
wife sucks dick / a vacuum with lips / does not choke /
on the oil-spill orgasm / the ideal wife / bends over /
takes every lie / the ideal wife is / a blow up doll / with
warm flesh / the ideal wife is / a lump of clay / for you /
to mold

{where is the bar set}

For the mothers:

here is this pole vault your first hurdle will be your changing
body but don't forget not to gain an inch of baby weight the
next step is to figure out how to care for this newborn human
with zero support are you keeping up with me pick up your
pace you will have to do the laundry plan the pediatrician
appointments don't forget to attend your own appointment
you want to make sure you're cleared to fuck by week six did
you see the overflowing dishes in the sink those are for you as
well you'll get funneled back to work before your organs are
fully back in their proper places also don't forget that breast is
best it will be implied everywhere that you're considered less
of a woman for choosing otherwise i hope your chapped and
cracked nipples like to be licked sensually you can't deny your
man his needs don't forget to eat healthy you better cook
every meal also do you know that your friends will disappear
because they think kids are boring or annoying do you know
that even though your brain body and soul have changed
drastically over the past ten months no one will care enough to
give you grace for it is your pole vault ready should i have
warned you that the judges are going to give you zeroes across
the board no matter what you do enjoy every moment it goes
so fast

For the fathers:

> here's a cigar! you stepped up to the
> plate!

do you wanna' play limbo?

(how low can we go)

{asking for a friend}

why do men   respect a ring   on a finger
more than   the woman   standing in   front
          of them   wearing it?

{fight / flight}
Erasure of The Used

I try to hold it all inside
But

I'm screaming

ode to coffee / 1

you are my scrying bowl
every morning sweetened

& softened for my esophageal
slip-and-slide the fall to the

cavern of my empty stomach
every morning feels like the

first drop on a rollercoaster

welcome to the big tent

the woman expands her body
to fit another human inside of it

like a circus tent only the elephant
in the room is her swollen belly &

the ringleader disappeared
like a cheap trick but she

gracefully steps into her new role
like a performance costume

she has always known
it all feels like tight-rope

walking without the net below
the ground flaming with

scattered targets she is terrified
of missing her mark will it all

come naturally like they say
she looks down & remembers

she's afraid of heights

elegy for the trophy wife

/ are we /

/ nothing /

/ more than /

/ a prize in /

/ a competition /

/ another object to /

/ put their hands on /

/ why are /

/ the wives /

/ the half /

/ to be shelved /

/ PPD /
Erasure of The Used

                              inside, I   am empty

I'm

                    pretending I'm not

I'll be   fine pretending

I'll be   fine,

I'll be just fine

a friendly reminder

ex·ploi·ta·tion

[ek-sploiˈ-tāSHən]

NOUN

1. the action or fact of treating someone unfairly in order to benefit from their work:

ex. watching your partner spin like a top towards the edge of her sanity raising the kids, cleaning the house, teaching you to be an adult, while being the main provider for the family

2. the fact of making use of a situation to gain unfair advantage for oneself:

ex. conveniently forgetting or overlooking any household chore until she's yelling like a banshee through the graveyard home you share

similar definitions include:

- manchild
- manipulation
- weaponized incompetence

ode to mom guilt

you sly fox you scissored-tongue devil you know exactly
what to say to me you know how to breathe down my
neck until i can't take it anymore you have this strange
way of sticking to my memory like toffee to my teeth
sometimes i think you will be the lover to lick me down
to my marrow you keep me up at night but i wake up
every morning trying to be better because of you

{a silent prayer}

A Memphis Mayfire Erasure

They said it gets easier, but they lied

I ask myself How am I supposed to be everything they expect me to be?

it doesn't feel like I'm living my dreams I know they say that no one is perfect, but

I feel so alone

I need   to change the inside of me   for their sake

God, give me the strength to do what you created me to do

ode to the only child

you took on the challenge of bearing
the weight of both sides of your family

lines from birth like a farmhand's
oxen it seems you were born

to carry the heavy responsibilities
misguided missiles for parents you

had no sibling to share
the craters they left behind but

you had dogs—maybe they
sensed there was a wolf in

you scare us all
how you go through life

without a pack to follow

they say inside of everyone

are two wolves at war &

if that's the case i think the reason

people fear you

came upon the two beasts

in the snow you stripped

yourself bare placed each

hand in a circle around your

snout howled at the moon

in unison the misunderstood creatures

danced under the glowing starlight

gossip // girl

do you ever wonder why your boss tells you that you
can't discuss your wages at work what would be the
point of that do you ever think about what life was like
before modern civilization how we all lived in these
village-like communities and the men would leave for
months on end trying to be silent while chasing tails and
then the women would be taking care of the village the
children the homes the hearths the women would be
making and mending clothes and gathering water and
berries nuts and honey the girls would be helping their
mothers and the children would all be watched over by
every mother when the men would return and the
women would lie with them and listen to their stories
about the plains and the mountains and the ocean the
women would take notes and every day by the river they
would share the knowledge amongst each other giggling
and braiding hair and one day we were told that our
fellow sisters were dangerous witches they called us
witches they made us and witches they burned us and we
have become fearful beings ever since now we compare
belt sizes and we throw shade and we spill tea but when
did we stop caring if a child gets to eat

# of mice & mothers

i left crackers & crumbs
hidden behind the vinegar

& oil bottles an effort to
make amends for all the lives

hurt while i turned a blind eye
isn't that the most universal

drive for us parents the need
to provide for our offspring

i wonder when i will gather
the courage to tell my husband

i have never liked killing a soul
that lives differently than we do

ode to coffee // 2

you smell like nostalgia younger than the first half of a
clock's face & i love when the scent brings me back to a
fuzzy memory the soft padding of my feet up the stairs or
down a hall or around a corner turning to see my mom
standing in the kitchen or sitting at the table or on the
couch & i can curl up into her lap like a kitten requesting
attention small soft & innocent the smell of roasted beans
unfurling like outreaching hands from her full cup

hormones & hemorrhoids

i think those are the biggest surprises that few mothers
decide to tell prospective mothers about and though they
are not fun topics a heads up would have been nice i
think the runner up on surprises would be the way all
your fears come rising to the surface of your psyche like
they suddenly found a way to breathe on land do you
ever think about when you were a teenager and you tried
to drown out your parents' voices with your upturned
music only to realize your throat holds their same melody
when you speak to your own genetic extensions when
did my voice get so loud when did it get so full of fear
when did it change in the first place was there a moment
in time when it just clicked over like a light switch on a
wall how did i not see i've been fumbling around in the
dark

ode to the firstborn

you impatient & brave leaf
falling from the tree still

tinged green you taught
me what it felt like to

swallow molten bronze &
i have not stopped burning since

while you were extracted from
the temple i find myself in

i held my oxygen i laid
like a pile of fortune-telling

bones silently praying
the years of vandalism

would not be held against

me i was never certain if

i was left with a tomb instead

{i'm scared i'm} sinking

Erasure of Em Beihold

I   feel

               too much

      the world, it feels too big

               bound to break

Snap my psyche like a twig

Do you ever get   tired of life?

Like you're not   happy,   you   wanna die

     you're hanging by a thread, but you   survive

              but you're not really there

          inside,

Like you're   out of love,

Am I past repair?

I wish that I could

make me happy

tired of trying to care
tired of quick repairs to cope
tired of sinking, there's water in my boat
I'm   trying to stay afloat

gamble

i've loved you since the moment i first met you.

& no, that's not a pick-up line, i saw the sisters of Fate
sew our lives together with red cord, by the 7th grade
lockers, forest-green & squeezed together like all the
skinny teenage girls trying to wear the hip-hugging
Dickie's pants that were popular in the body-shaming-era
that was 2006.

your hair grew upwards like broccoli & though i wasn't a
big fan of vegetables, that's the day i became obsessed
with dark, curly hair. & that puka shell necklace with that
bad boy attitude—it made my 13-year-old heart swoon.
our first kiss, i felt your braces behind your lips. i've had a
thing for crooked smiles ever since.

the truth is, i saw your sadness before the mahogany
freckle in your eye. it mirrored my own. i fell in love
with the broken boy before me & i've been trying to
piece you back together with parts of me.

& maybe, years later when we were grown adults trying
to fit like puzzle pieces, i was afraid we might be bent
into shapes that put us on opposite sides of the board.
maybe i chose to ignore it, like the oncoming train as i
tied myself to the tracks to show you, i would love you
no matter what way you chose to split me apart.

maybe i chose you because i thought you were the safe choice, a man that had shown me he would put his frustrated hands on controllers & not on me. i realize now, no man is a safe choice. it's a gamble no matter what, like we are all playing the game of love in a shitty casino, no clocks, no windows, & we're all out of luck.

elegy for my trust

it was the   week of   my dad's funeral
     when i found out   the picture   of
her   smiling up   at me   your   unlocked
     phone turned confessional   holding   a
nun   in a lace   push-up bra
     praying   the   Father
     would be   tempted   to grab
        a handful   a single swipe up   to
confirm   like the crime scene photo
     wasn't enough   each   digital love
     letter sliced my aorta   like   a
     freshly sharpened   claymore   to   a
bare back   this stab   left   a
gaping hole   inside of   the cranium
     attached to   my spine   a towering
     Redwood   fell   to its knees   I heard
        something   snap
   that   no   one else   seemed
   to   i wanted   to   call
   my dad   that day   to ask
   him   if   he had   any
   words of   wisdom   for me but
   to   my   recollection there are   no
   payphones   in   paradise

"letting herself go"

really means the men don't want to fuck her anymore

really means the women are afraid of looking like her

really means that she curses to herself about her body not being a glorified sex-toy

really means that she smiles when she wants to cry

really means that she prioritizes everyone but herself

ode to drive-thru coffee shops

energy levels down to critical levels i locate the nearest
mana refill station i tote three important passengers in my
midnight hued metal beast these small passengers speak a
language i do not quite understand but i try to facilitate
meanings with hand gestures for they have short tempers
and i fear for their extreme reactions at times ice falls and
i speak to the mages that create these healing tonics after
an exchange of coin for their time and materials they
recede into their place of magic and i try to soothe the
angry trifecta behind me i realize i have remnants from
the battle over the dreaded tissue paper on my shoulder a
green glob now dried i think to myself i must look like a
goblin in my current state then suddenly the exquisite
potion is in my hands i ride away the air behind us is
filled with the screams of these three tiny goblins i
chauffeur i sip the beverage and for a brief sparkling
moment i no longer care that i am covered in goop while
parading around town

elegy for the sunken mothers

girls are taught how to put on a painted face how to
pretend their smile does not carry secrets behind its teeth
the girls are taught how to use their hands for beauty
regimes rather than waving a white flag they are not
taught that those same hands will shake them awake each
night explaining that Anxiety & Fear were trying to
submerge them in their sleep the girls are not taught that
they are expected to become life rafts that they will have
to keep their heads above water without ever learning
how to swim the girls are not taught how to tread water
how to keep themselves from getting pulled to the depths
below the girls that grow into women that become
mothers that sink like concrete blocks they are left
forever holding in their screams as if it was their fault that
they were thrown into a body that felt like the lead in a
pencil stone-cold waiting for someone to see the dark pit
of despair that was drawing up the map of their future
how it always led to their end how they wished for one
single beam to cut through the darkness a lighthouse to
lead them away from the ghost ship of themselves how
they begged to be seen from the cliff's edge how these
mothers breathlessly prayed for anyone to see that they
were struggling all along

ode to the middle child

// before you were a reality // i dreamt of you //
prophetic princess with curls // gifted a crown of third
eyes // i hope to teach you // to never question your
intuition // & to always spit out kernels of jealousy //
like sunflower seed shells // i always swallowed them
whole //

if "God" is dead

i'm sure it's because She worked Herself to Death

i'm sure Her male counterpart was able to take the credit after that

i'm sure He became a jealous and spiteful "God"— created war, famine, greed

But i'm also sure if we were made in Her image, we have the power to create a better world

in praise of the women in Iceland

After October 24ᵗʰ, 1975

the women in Iceland know how to make a point by
walking straight out the door leaving husbands to figure
out how to work an oven fathers to care for their
children while the news was being read aloud on the
radio children were heard playing in the background men
answering the phone at home to be interviewed by the
newscasters while their wives marched arm in arm with
their fellow sisters and mothers and daughters these
women linked together by the realization they were the
damn reason the country was able to run itself in the first
place the men did not retaliate the men thanked their
wives by voting for a single and divorced mother as their
president in 1980 the women in Iceland taught the world
a lesson and we all fell asleep in class

ode to the third child

/// your arrival was /// an unexpected gift /// from a
goddess herself /// you were named after her /// born
into a full family /// you have only known /// a warm
home with /// the hum of other steps /// & words &
songs /// i see healing /// with your arrival /// the
future led by /// a generation of Valkyrie /// children
sent from /// the heavens above to /// save this world
from /// the devils destroying it ///

ode to coffee /// 3

/ most parents / say that tea / is the best remedy / for
any illness / a little honey / a little lemon / when i was
younger / my dad / wouldn't let me / drink caffeine /
but when i would get sick / he would / always brew /
up a batch / of Folger's / & he always used / the lactose-
free powdered creamer / & if you've ever tasted that taste
/ you'll know the sweetness / hints its artificial
tendencies / the powder sticking / to the sides of the
mug / like snowflakes / to upheld tongues / & despite
the crusty / entry to my lips / i would always relish / in
the moment / my dad / handing me this warm gift / &
now / when i am sick / all i can think of / to make me /
feel better / is those two / hands / holding a fresh cup /
of coffee / & passing it / to me /

in praise of the mom bun

a secret therapist inside of the crown on my head
listening to every song i play on repeat to squeeze
serotonin into my eardrums you don't mind when you
become a bird's home harboring nested emotions deep
blue wings clipped & stuffed into thin shells to later be
scattered around the floorboards embracing my head
every time rivers stream into satin covered feathers the
most gentle smothering you are the most loyal friend i
have ever known when i'm sick you're there to hold my
hair back from the exorcism of my bowels when i'm
rushing out the door you're there to help me pretend i
had time to get ready when i was younger i would
imagine having babies at the same time as my best friends
so we could embark through motherhood together but
i've been on this journey with only my shadow as
company so far and when i see my outline i see you no
matter what i know you'll always be there to hold my
head up when i want to hang it low

revisiting the women in Iceland

After October 24th, 2023

the women in Iceland ████████████████
███████████████████████ ████████████
████████████████████████████████████
████████████████ ██████████████████████
███████████ heard ████████████████ men
answering █████████████████ to ████████
██████████ their wives ██████ arm in arm ████
████████████████████████████████████
████████ linked together by the realization they were the
damn ████████ country ██████████████████
████████████████████████████████████
████████████████████████████████████
████████████████████████

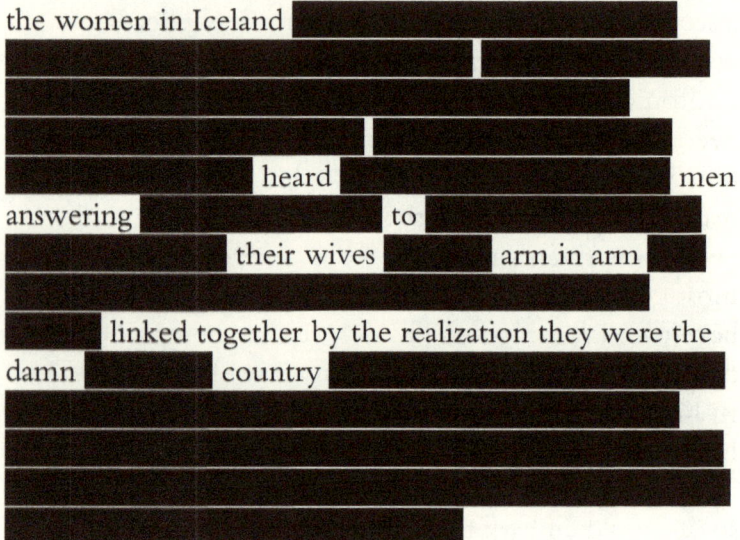

the women in Iceland are fighting for equal rights in the
country voted as the world's most gender-equal country
what does that say for the richest country in the world
with the largest wage gap in recorded history what does
that say about the country taking away human rights
from its own citizens

in praise of the other girl

i can see what he saw
in you you're beautiful

beyond words & trust
me i know words well

you are a honeysuckle soft
sweet naturally provided

with the law of attraction i
am a false rose of Jericho

dried up abrasive round
ball of desert moss gifted

with resurrection & you
darling taught me that i

can bring myself back to life

one final reminder (to stay)

A Sinead O'Connor Erasure

It's been so lonely without you here
Like a bird without a song

All the flowers that you planted mama
In the back yard
All died when you went away

Nothing

compares

to you

exploited labor

have you heard of the term invisible labor (women) the silent backbone of society for every generation since the birth of patriarchal society (women) supporting men behind closed doors in their careers by doing housework preparing and cooking meals making sure groceries are stocked keeping finances in order planning doctor appointments filling out school enrollment paperwork (women) taking care of children and even when abandoned forced to take every responsibility upon our shoulders even if it's being the blame

★★★

do you know what it is like to feel the fear associated with knowing you have less of a chance of survival due to the possibility of being hunted down quietly what it's like to look over your shoulder whenever you are alone or simply not walking with XY chromosomes if or when you are raped you can become pregnant i would like all the straight men in the room to imagine being raped by a malicious alien and then having its spawn rip out of you months later i bet if aliens walked amongst us in the shadows targeted men for their sexual appetites and reproduction purposes abortion laws would be pretty fucking lenient

★★★

imagine / if this is how / a suburban housewife feels / what do you think / the women growing and harvesting

our organic produce / the women mining for cobalt to
create our latest version of smart device / the women
sweating over threads for our fashion / feel like

acknowledgements

first and foremost, i have to thank my loving family unit for supporting me and loving me during this journey.

i would not have made it this far had it not been for the four of you. Conor, Cairo, Zelda and Freya, you all are my entire universe. living this life with you all is my greatest joy.

Conor, my love, i am so grateful to share this life with you. thank you for healing with me. thank you for supporting me, always. thank you for pushing me to share my words.

thank you to every fellow writer that i have shared space with, during writing workshops and poetry readings.

thank you to every true friend that has supported me during this journey. i am extremely grateful to have you in my life.

thank you to all my English teachers over the years, and to my journalism teacher in high school.

thank you to my parents for creating me and guiding me the best you could.

thank you to the following in no particular order: my dog Vash books nintendo tarot mascara runes Edgar Allan Poe my intuition tiktok coffee writing workshops fall out boy dollar stores Fate love bookstores the color black

tattoos dr. marten's parmesan cheese chocolate notebooks
& pens that actually work when you need them to

about the author

Amber Awni is a poet, writer, and editor from the United States—also a mother and wife, Amber writes full-time while managing a household for five.

Follow Amber Awni on her writing journey:

Instagram @thelegendofamber

TikTok @amberawni

Follow Rainbow Raven Publishing:

Instagram @rainbowravenpublishingllc

TikTok: @rainbow.raven.pub